D0230359

Oxfam would like to acknowledge, with thanks, the following photographers:
Amin from the Drik Photo Agency (pages 8-9), Annie Bungeroth (pages 6-7, 12-13, 16-17,
cover and back cover), Caroline Irby (pages 24-25), Geoff Sayer (pages 26-27),
Rajendra Shaw (pages 22-23) and Sungwan So (pages 14-15).

First published in Great Britain in 2010 by
Frances Lincoln Children's Books, 4 Torriano Mews,
Torriano Avenue, London NW5 2RZ
www.franceslincoln.com

ISBN 978-1-84507-974-1

Set in ITC Stone Sans and Providence Sans

Printed in Heshan, Guangdong, China by Leo Paper Products Ltd. in April 2010

1 3 5 7 9 8 6 4 2

Oxfam GB will receive a 5% royalty for each copy of this book sold in the UK.

Our Animals

F
FRANCES LINCOLN
CHILDREN'S BOOKS

in association with  **Oxfam**

Isabela is carrying
a cockerel to the market.
She is from a village of
people called Mayans
in Guatemala.

This cockerel
is nearly as
big as me!

Saran's family have a
farm in Bangladesh.
He has rescued this injured
pigeon from drowning.

I take care of
the pigeons on
our farm.

Shanyi and her family are feeding the carp at this traditional Chinese garden.

I've never seen so many fish!

Gamachu belongs to the Borana people in Ethiopia, who keep camels, as well as cattle, goats and sheep.

Camels are very grumpy!

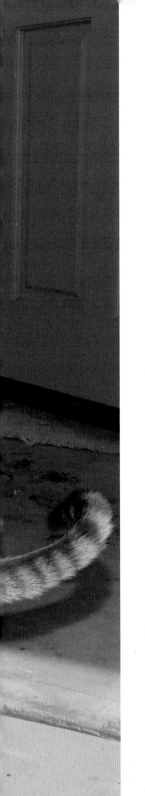

Dahlys's family has two cats and two goldfish in their home in California, in the United States of America.

My cat is very thirsty!

Lucas's family farm alpacas for their wool in the mountains of Peru.

My hat and jumper are made from alpaca wool.

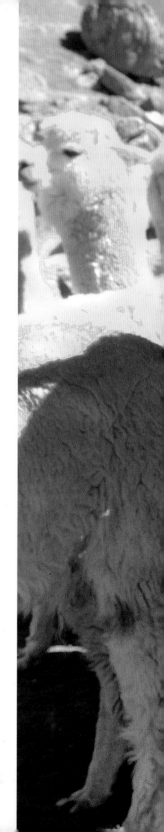

This girl's family breeds rabbits on their farm in a Moroccan village.

These boys from the Munduruku Indian tribe in Brazil love their pet pig.

She likes it when we scratch her tummy.

This girl is helping her
mother feed their geese.
They live in India.

I hope it
doesn't peck
my fingers!

There is no running water in Barfimoh's village in Tajikistan, so she rides her donkey to collect water from a spring.

The containers are too heavy for me to carry on my own.

Khadija has just met this goat kid on a visit to a farm in Tekane, Mauritania.

USA

Morocco

Guatemala

Peru

Mauritania

Brazil

Tajikistan

Ethiopia

China

Bangladesh

India

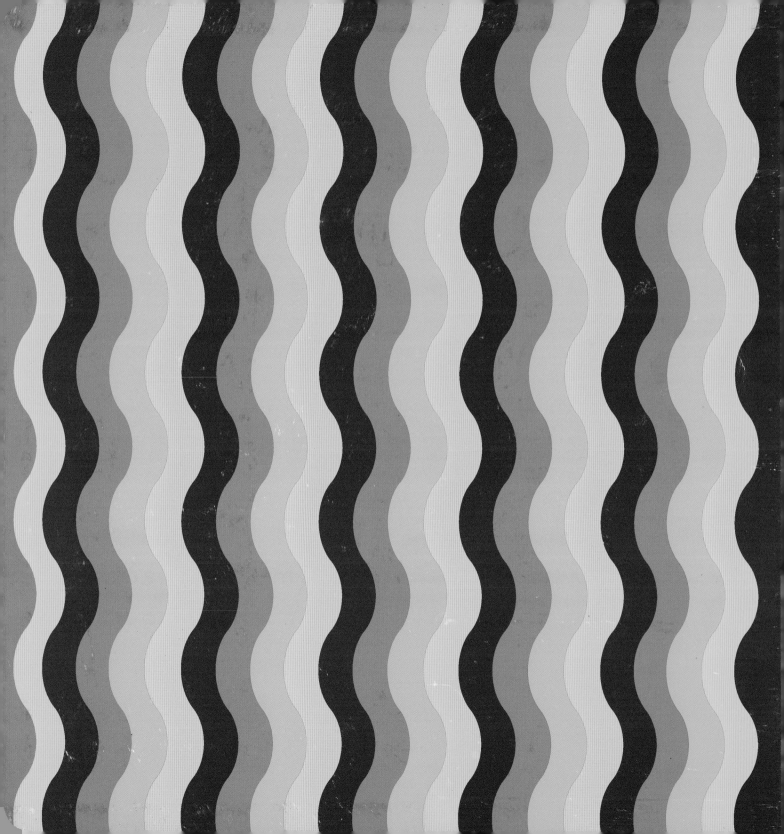